Original title:
Threads of a Story

Copyright © 2025 Creative Arts Management OÜ
All rights reserved.

Author: Adrian Caldwell
ISBN HARDBACK: 978-1-80586-112-6
ISBN PAPERBACK: 978-1-80586-584-1

The Binding of Legends

In a land where socks went missing,
And pants would purposely shrink,
There lived a tale of quirky beings,
Who whispered secrets over a drink.

A turtle raced a rabbit one day,
With carrots as a prize, no less,
But the turtle took a nap, they say,
Leaving the crowd in sheer distress.

A hero found a magic shoelace,
To tie his dreams with perfect knots,
But every time he'd try to race,
He'd trip and fall in silly spots.

The dragon's breath was sweet like pie,
He baked cakes that flew through the sky,
Yet, every slice would twist and twirl,
Leaving the diners in a whirl.

So gather 'round and laugh with glee,
For every tale is slightly bent,
In the world of whimsy and folly,
Each silly moment is heaven-sent.

The Binding of Experiences

In a coffee shop, a sip too hot,
I accidentally spilled, oh what a plot!
With laughter shared, we wiped the floor,
While our caffeine dreams flew out the door.

The cat on the counter, quite the show,
Swiped my muffin, oh no, oh no!
We laughed till we cried, all over crumbs,
In this funny tale, my heart just hums.

A Cloth of Whimsy

With socks mismatched and shoes awry,
I danced like a flamingo, oh me, oh my!
The postman blinked, my neighbors laughed,
As I twirled around like a fabric craft.

A kite flew by, caught in a breeze,
Tugged my unruly hair with such ease.
I chased it down, a race to win,
But tripped on a dog—oh, let the fun begin!

Colorful Strands of Lives

At the fair, I tried the crazy ride,
Squealed at the top, then lost my pride.
The cotton candy melted in my hand,
Like my dignity—oh, isn't life grand?

A man with a parrot joined the queue,
The bird squawked loudly; it didn't like blue!
We laughed with glee, shared popcorn in heaps,
While the parrot plotted some fuzzy leaps.

Stories That Mend

At grandma's house, we baked a pie,
Flour on noses, oh my, oh my!
The recipe called for salt, not sweet,
Now it's a dish for a sneeze-inspired treat.

Our dog snatched a slice, dashing out fast,
While we all just wondered how long this would last.
With laughter unbound and giggles that blend,
In the mess of our stories, we find a good friend.

Interwoven Lives

In a world where socks do roam,
A missing pair is never home.
Cats play tug with yarn so bold,
Grandpa's tales are always gold.

Neighbors compete in bake-off feats,
With cupcakes shaped like tiny feet.
Laughter rings in every bite,
As frosting splatters take to flight.

Fables in Fabric

Once lived a shirt with stripes so bright,
It lost a button in a fight.
Its buddy PJs had a groove,
They danced at night, the perfect move.

The shorts got jealous, started whine,
Claimed they were cooler, oh so fine.
But when the rain began to pour,
The shorts just shrieked, 'We can't take more!'

Woven Silhouettes

In a closet lived some shoes,
Who argued over daily views.
One was tall, the other flat,
They'd bicker, but they loved to chat.

A scarf once tangled in a game,
Claimed fashion's always to blame.
It ended up in quite a twist,
A fashion faux pas on the list!

Threads of Existence

A button popped off with a spree,
It found a life as a frisbee.
Laughter echoed down the lane,
As kids threw it, went insane.

A thread from pants danced in delight,
Reciting jokes that felt just right.
In fabric land, they thrive and cheer,
Each stitch a memory, oh so dear.

Kaleidoscope of Tangles

In a world where socks do hide,
Colors clash and patterns collide.
The cat wears one, the dog a shoe,
Every morning feels like a zoo.

Jumbled jokes in mismatched pairs,
A teddy bear treads without cares.
Spaghetti strings and lost balloons,
Welcome to my life of cartoons.

Narrative Weavings

Once a squirrel stole my lunch,
I chased it down, got quite the hunch.
It clung to a branch, fruits held tight,
While I turned red and felt the fright.

Stories linger in silly spots,
Like peanut butter on my socks.
Each memory wrapped in a giggle,
Life's too short, so let's just wiggle.

Hidden Stories Beneath

Beneath my bed, the shoes conspire,
They plot to run, oh, how they tire.
Each pair has tales of mud and funk,
Adventures lived in the deep dark junk.

Dust bunnies dance in a lively waltz,
Disguised as fluff, they are no false.
Whispers echo of snacks once dropped,
In the realm where chaos never stopped.

A Tapestry of Heartstrings

A puppy's joy and a cake gone wrong,
 Baker's bliss sings a funny song.
 Eggs are scrambled, frosting's a beast,
 This kitchen circus has quite the feast.

Grandpa's tales with a wink and a nudge,
 Turn serious moments into a grudge.
 Life's a patchwork of giggles and sighs,
 In this carnival, laughter never dies.

Connected by Stitches

In a quilt of quirks we unite,
With mismatched socks and dreams in flight.
Every patch tells tales, so absurd,
Of the cat who thinks it's a circus bird.

With a needle of laughter we poke and prod,
Creating a mess, it's all a bit broad.
Sewing up memories, tight like our pants,
In this fabric of fun, we all do a dance.

The Weaving of Us

With yarns of joy, we spin our fate,
Mismatched tales that make us wait.
Oh, the knots we tie in silly ways,
Like grandma's jokes from her younger days.

We weave in laughter, pull out the fuss,
As tangled as our love for this bus.
Riding along, we stitch and squeal,
A tapestry bright, outrageous and real.

The Fabric of Connection

In a tapestry spun of giggles and glee,
Our stories entwined, not always free.
With colors that clash, yet somehow it works,
Like a dance of the socks when the dryer jerks.

Stitch by stitch, we patch up our tales,
With laughter that sprinkles like holiday sales.
This fabric is funky, but oh so divine,
Woven together, like cheese and a fine wine.

Cords of Reminiscence

With cords of laughs, we reminisce,
Creating a bondage that's hard to miss.
Each loop's a story, each twist a cheer,
Like the time we lost the cat for a year.

In the fibers of memory, the fun never ends,
As we tug on the strings, oh how it bends.
A tapestry wild, a circus of joy,
With every weird knot, we find a new ploy.

The Interlace of Truth

In a fabric shop, truth did sit,
Looking for a perfect knit.
It unraveled, much to its plight,
Said, "This yarn just ain't right!"

A piece of lace joined the mix,
With gossip and scandal, oh what a fix!
The buttons chimed in, with tales quite bold,
While seams whispered secrets, terribly old.

Colors of a Journey

A red sock lost on a road so blue,
Met a yellow shoe, who just flew.
Together they laughed, a colorful bunch,
Planning to have a remarkable lunch!

They painted the town in stripes and dots,
Tripping on trips, and laughing a lot.
Each hue brought laughter to stories they spun,
In the end, a riotous blend just for fun.

The Knit of Life

With needles clicking, a life began,
Stitching together the plan of the man.
Dropped a stitch, the cat took a leap,
Said, "I prefer a cozy sleep!"

The scarf grew long, with tales of woe,
A patchwork of dreams in every row.
Yet every unravel brought giggles, you see,
Life's a knit, filled with comedy!

Shadows in the Loom

In a loom of shadows, a spider did weave,
Making patterns that made folks believe.
But alas, a breeze did come blow,
And the masterpiece? Just a tangled show!

The worms all whispered, "What a grand show!"
While hints of colors began to glow.
Each twist and turn brought hilarious flares,
In the loom of laughter, nobody cares!

The Loom of Life

In the loom of life, we weave our fate,
Each day a stitch, can't be late.
With laughter bright and mishaps bold,
Our tales unfold like yarns of gold.

A cat walks by, tangles the thread,
Socks go missing, that's what I dread.
Grandma's tales, they twist and bend,
In the end, we all descend!

Echoes in the Weave

In echoes of laughter, we find the plot,
Knitting odd socks from the things we've bought.
A hat for the dog? Now that's a tale,
It's not very smart, but it sure won't fail!

A needle slips, creation's lost,
But who really cares about the cost?
With each little hiccup, we dance and shake,
For life's a patchwork, make no mistake!

Patterns of the Past

Patterns of past, all wobbly and wrong,
A patch here and there, nothing too strong.
With mismatched colors, we try our best,
Like a quilt made by a caffeinated guest.

A drop of jam, oh what a mess,
A story of clumsiness to confess.
But each silly moment makes a great laugh,
Like a wobbly chair, it's the best of the craft!

Fabricated Dreams

In fabricated dreams, we stitch up the fun,
A t-shirt that says, "I'm the Uncle of One!"
With mischief and giggles, we plot and plan,
To make the best tales, yes, yes we can!

So here's to the whimsies, wavy and bright,
With buttons askew, we dance through the night.
Let's weave our laughter into the seam,
For life's just a fabric of wild, crazy dreams!

Echoing Patterns

In a land where socks go rogue,
Dancing daily on the logs.
They paint a path with giggles loud,
While shoes all sigh beneath the clouds.

A cat named Whiskers plays the fool,
He hides the yarn, oh what a rule!
The dog chases, slips, and slides,
As laughter in the garden bides.

Where mismatched mittens share their tales,
Of snowy days and paper trails.
Each stitch of life a playful jest,
In this odd tapestry, we're blessed.

Life's Fabricated Tales

Once a turtle dreamed of speed,
While her friends just laughed, indeed.
With a rocket strapped on tight,
She zoomed away, oh what a sight!

A bumblebee with a funny hat,
Buzzed around, oh imagine that!
He claimed he'd break the world's flight,
But tripped on flowers, what a fright!

In the corner, a hamster spins,
Telling tales where no one wins.
His wheel of stories going round,
In laughter's grip, we all are bound.

The Abode of Woven Wishes

In a house where dreams collide,
A couch where giggles love to hide.
There's a cat in a pirate's cape,
Plotting to steal the fishy grape.

A chandelier of jellybeans,
Where humor lands and laughter beams.
The curtains sing in playful tunes,
While shadows dance beneath the moon.

In this abode of wishes bright,
Every corner sparks delight.
With stories spun in twinkling lights,
Here joy endures, day and night.

Layers of Lived Experience

In layers thick of joy and jest,
A wise old man had quite the quest.
He folded hats into grand shapes,
Pretending to be ships with scrapes.

A girl with dreams of ice cream lands,
Made castles high with her small hands.
Each scoop a giggle, every cone,
Became a tale that's widely known.

With every layer, laughter grows,
In quirky tales, hilarity flows.
We weave our lives in colors bold,
In funny stories, we unfold.

Tapestry of Tales

Once a cat wore a hat, so grand,
It danced with a mouse, quite unplanned.
They twirled on the floor, made a fuss,
While the dog just sighed, "This ain't for us."

The elephant sang a tune offbeat,
While a parrot squawked, "Hey, that's neat!"
A kangaroo joined with a hop and a jig,
While the crowd laughed hard at the scene so big.

The Fabric of Memory

Grandpa's old tales spun round and round,
Of a chicken that flew and never touched ground.
The cow jumped over moons, or so he'd claim,
With the rooster as pilot, oh what a game!

A caped grandma zoomed in her chair,
Defeating the laundry monster with flair.
She'd laugh and she'd sing, a sight to behold,
In a house full of stories, all silly and bold.

Unraveled Narratives

In a town where socks lost their pairs,
People wore mismatches without their cares.
A purple and green, blue and a stripe,
Fashion rebels danced, like a wild type.

The dog wore a vest as fine as gold,
You'd think he was royalty, so brave, so bold.
But he tripped on his tail, fell right on his face,
And the cats laughed out loud, oh what a disgrace!

Strands of Connection

A fish told a tale of the land so dry,
It wished it could leap, touch the bright sky.
So the frog made a plan, with a jump and a splash,
"Let's swap for a day, hope it's a fast crash!"

But the fish learned to swim with impressive grace,
While the frog wore a hat and put on a face.
Together they laughed, what a sight to see,
Just two silly friends, boundless and free.

The Needle's Path

In the workshop sat a needle so spry,
Dancing through fabric, a twinkle in its eye.
It stitched up a tale quite oddly absurd,
Of a squirrel who fancied himself quite the bird.

With thread all a tangle and knots in a spin,
The needle just laughed, 'Where do I begin?'
A patchwork of laughter, a quilt full of cheer,
As the stitches recounted a melodious fear.

A button once grumbled, 'I'm not for the show!'
But the needle just winked, 'You're a superstar, bro!'
With each little poke, there's a story unveiled,
Of adventures unfurling where laughter prevailed.

Patterns of Forgotten Dreams

In a cupboard of dreams, dust motes did waltz,
A quilt made of giggles and childhood faults.
Each patch told a story of trips gone awry,
Where birthdays turned sour but we laughed till we cried.

With polka dots swirling and stripes in a dash,
The fabric remembered a handsome mustache.
The toaster exploded while making French toast,
We all learned that breakfast could also be roast!

Mom's purse had the mystery of lost little toys,
Like rubbery monsters and odd little joys.
The patterns keep changing, yet laughter stays true,
In the fabric of life, there's always me and you.

Woven Realities

In the loom of a dreamland, where oddities blend,
A sock had a meeting with a hat that could bend.
They talked of adventures in fantastical lands,
While a t-shirt just giggled at their silly plans.

The patterns were wild, with colors so bright,
They twirled and they twisted deep into the night.
With each silly stitch, new quirks would emerge,
A scarf turned into a wild, snappy verge.

A tale of confusion, where mismatched things cheer,
An umbrella once tried to date a deer.
But no one seemed certain, quite how it would go,
In the fabric of life, laughter's the show.

The Cloth of Experience

There once was a blanket so cozy and wide,
It whispered of stories that giggled inside.
With patches of moments, all silly and bright,
It softens the tales of our day-to-day plight.

From pancake disasters to falling off bikes,
It captured our laughter and all the odd strikes.
A bandana chimed in with tales from the street,
Where clumsy met hiccups and friendship so sweet.

The seams held our secrets, all stitched with a grin,
Of pranks pulled on neighbors, and garden gnome kin.
In the fabric of living, no worries do cling,
For life's just a patchwork where joy's the main thing.

The Chronicle in Color

In a quilt worn thin and frayed,
Lie tales of naps and lemonade.
A cat that swipes the pizza slice,
Or grandma's sneeze, oh, what a price!

The socks on the wall had quite a chat,
One said, "Why am I on this mat?"
The goldfish sighed and took a dive,
For all these tales, we must survive!

A hamster wheel spun round and round,
While chubby squirrels danced abound.
A mismatch of life, it's quite absurd,
In this scribbled book, strange is the word!

Each color bright, a silly scene,
Where nothing's ever quite routine.
With a wink and a nod, let's take a chance,
In life's odd stories, let's laugh and dance!

Signs of Stitched Stories

When patches collide, it's quite a sight,
A button-eyed owl takes to flight.
With mismatched buttons on a coat,
You'd think it was made by a goat!

The dog thought he'd play fetch with socks,
But cats threw yarn and hoarded rocks.
The mailman tripped and fell on his rear,
With grass stains to show for his big career!

Every stitch tells a joke or two,
Like grandma's hat, all shades of blue.
With laughter stitched throughout each seam,
These quirky tales make life a dream!

Blankets billow with each silly tale,
Of pickle parties and singing snails.
In this bright patchwork, let's take a gander,
At stories funny that we all can squander!

Connecting the Dots

With dots and squiggles, what a mess,
A rabbit in pants who loves to confess.
He danced with frogs in a top hat grand,
While jellybeans were in high demand!

The pencil pounced like a feline cat,
Doodling shapes of cheese and a hat.
A crayon wars with a watercolor,
Creating chaos, and oh, what a splatter!

We join the dots, a shape unfolds,
A tale of ice cream that never grows old.
But wait, a pickle joins the scene,
In this wild drawing, nothing's routine!

So grab a crayon, don't be shy,
Let's color this tale and aim high.
With laughter in lines, let's scribble and rhyme,
For every dot leads to fun every time!

The Art of Narrative Weaving

In Grandma's loom, she sings aloud,
A tapestry made to charm the crowd.
With tales of frogs in polka dots,
And socks that dance in coffee pots!

The threads of humor twine and twist,
Crafting stories you won't want to miss.
A chicken that juggles and rides a bike,
Now that's the kind of tale we like!

As looms creak softly like an old tune,
Woven tales embrace the afternoon.
With each silly strand that we create,
Life becomes fun, there's no debate!

So let us spin these stories bright,
With laughter woven in pure delight.
For in this fabric of fun and cheer,
The best of tales are always near!

The Patchwork Chronicle

Once a cat wore a lovely hat,
But it flew off and landed flat.
It landed on a dog's nose,
And caused him to sneeze, oh how it rose!

The hat took off like a paper plane,
Chased by a squirrel, full of disdain.
They danced with a raccoon, oh such a sight,
In the park, twirling under the moonlight.

A bird snagged the hat in its beak,
But soon made a nest; it looked so chic!
Now the cat wears a new type of flair,
With feathers and leaf, it's a sight rare!

In this whimsical tale of chase and thrill,
Who knew that a hat could bring such a chill?
Laughter echoed wherever they'd roam,
In the lands of the goofy, they found a home!

Cords of Destiny

In a kitchen, a noodle danced with glee,
While a fork looked on, as proud as can be.
A spoon chimed in, "Why not join the waltz?"
But tangled spaghetti had its own faults!

They twirled and spun, oh what a mess!
With sauce flying, it was anyone's guess.
A pot boiled over, causing great alarm,
While a ladle tried hard to keep calm.

The chef walked in, eyes wide and agog,
As his dinner was now a pasta fog.
Yet laughter erupted, no one was mad,
For a kitchen fiasco can't be that bad!

So they raised their forks, a toast to the fun,
With sticky sweet chaos, they'd all won.
In every twist and turn, they found delight,
As noodles danced on through the night!

The Yarn of Years

Once a ball of yarn rolled down the hall,
Chasing a mouse, it began to sprawl.
The mouse giggled, running quick and fast,
While the yarn got tangled, not built to last.

A puppy joined in, barking with flair,
To catch that yarn and give it a scare.
They tumbled together, a loop-de-loop,
The cat watched on, plotting to scoop!

In a comical race, the yarn made a dash,
But a nearby chair turned it into a crash.
With fluff in the air, it turned into art,
While laughter erupted, oh where to start!

So they rolled and they tossed, in a joyful spree,
A tale woven with giggles, as fun as can be.
For no matter the yarn, or the chase it incites,
It's all in good fun, our hearts take flight!

Twisted Echoes

In a town where the wind howled low,
Lived a parrot with quite the show.
He'd mimic all folks, leave them in stitches,
With silly sounds and wild little glitches.

One day he heard an odd noise indeed,
A goose honked back, oh how he'd lead!
They formed a duet, a song quite absurd,
As they laughed and danced, no one was perturbed.

The mailman arrived, and what did he find?
A chorus of honks, and a parrot intertwined!
He chuckled aloud, lost in their fun,
As the town echoed laughter, a day well begun.

Now whenever the wind sings through those streets,
You can hear echoes of their whimsical feats.
With the parrot and goose and the jolly mail,
Life's just a giggle, when shared without fail!

Patchwork Prose

Once a tale was stitched with care,
A sock, a hat, a flavor rare.
The grandma quipped, 'Oh, it's a mess!
But isn't chaos just the best?'

In patchwork lands, the cats would dance,
Wearing shoes, they took a chance.
The cows joined in with such great flair,
Singing songs that filled the air.

A stitch or two began to fray,
As laughter bloomed throughout the day.
With needles twirled, the words took flight,
Creating giggles through the night.

So grab a patch or two, my friend,
Let's write a tale that twists and bends.
For every slip leads to a new,
And quirky twist, just like a shoe.

Weavings of the Mind

In the loom of thought, a mishmash spun,
With spaghetti thoughts and puns for fun.
A brain so tangled, a wild parade,
Of quirky characters, all hand-made.

A baker danced in fluffy shoes,
Mixing batters for silly brews.
The recipe called for a pinch of cheer,
And a whole lot of giggles, never fear!

The toaster jumped and then it wobbled,
As coffee pots just giggled and gobbled.
In this wild web, no tale is plain,
Just quirky quirks and a touch of rain.

So come, let's join this wild surprise,
In the weavings where the laughter flies.
With minds entwined, we craft anew,
A zany story, just me and you!

Harmonics of a Narrative

A fiddler played a tale so bright,
Each note a chuckle, pure delight.
The squirrels tapped their tiny feet,
Creating rhythms on the street.

As hats and shoes began to spin,
A chicken clucked, 'Let's all join in!'
The giggles grew, a merry band,
Under the shade of a jellybean stand.

The melody twisted, high and low,
With every quirk, another show.
The chorus sang, a humorous quest,
In this vibrant jest, we felt so blessed.

So grab your friends, and let's compose,
A symphony where laughter flows.
For in this dance of word and rhyme,
We'll craft a tale that beats in time.

Embroidered Journeys

Upon a road with stitches fine,
A funny tale we tried to entwine.
With each tiny knot, a giggle grew,
As mismatched travelers drew the cue.

A penguin rode a bicycle, too,
Wearing a scarf of bright sky blue.
The elephants danced in matching socks,
While time ticked by like silly clocks.

We spun our yarns of odd delight,
The sun shining down, so warm and bright.
Our laughter echoed through the lanes,
Each silly step, one less to strain.

So take a stitch, come walk with me,
On this journey, wild and free.
For every twist and turn we chase,
Holds a zany smile, a warm embrace.

Echoes Woven Together

In a cafe bright, a cat sits near,
She dangles strings, oh what a cheer!
A fly buzzes 'round, trying to flee,
While the cat just grins, 'Come play with me!'

A noodle slurps, what a goal!
A chef now juggles with a roll!
The pasta leaps, in a twisty move,
Eating its way, just to groove!

A dog with socks, can you believe?
Chased by kids who just won't leave.
They race and tumble, laughter erupts,
As spaghetti dreams of being wrapped up!

Suddenly, a grand old squirrel hops,
With peanut dreams, it never stops.
Together they spin, in silly sway,
Crafting joy, in their playful way!

A Tapestry of Echoes

A wise old owl wears glasses too,
Tells stories of dreams, as skies turn blue.
Swooping low, with a chuckle and hoot,
He makes wisecracks in his feathered suit.

In the corner, a bear eats cake,
With frosting on paws, what a mistake!
Laughter spills from friends in glee,
For nothing beats bear cake jubilee!

A rabbit hops in a polka-dot hat,
Juggling carrots while dancing flat.
His silly steps bring chuckles aplenty,
As he sneezes, "Oops! Just too many!"

So round they go, in a funny dance,
With giggles echoing, it's quite a chance.
The humor woven, oh what a blend,
In a night of tales that never end!

Stories in Silk

A spider spins silk, oh so bright,
Telling tales of the day and night.
A fly buzzes by, completely unaware,
His fate's wrapped in silk, oh what a scare!

A mouse in boots, with a sandwich slice,
Wanders through dreams, so very nice.
He meets a snail, so slow and sly,
"Want a ride?" he asks; the snail says "Why?"

They travel far on a whimsy quest,
But cheese and bread make them both rest.
With silly giggles and crumbs everywhere,
They plot their next snack with grand flair!

A worm pops up, with a wise old grin,
"Let's not forget, the joy is within!"
They laugh and munch, with joys that twine,
Creating moments that feel just fine!

Life's Intricate Weavings

There once was a frog with a flashy bow,
He croaked out tunes, putting on a show.
A crowd of bugs danced 'neath the moonlight,
While the frog sang songs, all silly and bright.

A turtle came by, slow and late,
He asked for a dance, but the rhythm's great.
With two left feet, he stumbled and twirled,
Causing a giggle across the whole world!

A cricket on stage with a spunky flair,
Took a big leap, sailing through the air.
He landed on daisies, with quite a flair,
"Who knew life could be so light as air?"

And so they wove their funny tale,
Of frogs and bugs, on a joyous trail.
In laughter's embrace, they twirled and spun,
Life's woven stories, just bursting with fun!

Frayed Ends of Fate

Once a sock lost, never to meet,
Hiding in laundry, oh what a feat!
With one foot cold and one warm delight,
Unraveled chaos, a comical sight.

A button rolled under the couch,
It spins and twirls like a little slouch.
Crisis of clothing, an epic tale,
When pants fall down, you just can't fail.

A zipper stuck like a fish on land,
I wrestle it back with an awkward hand.
Garments entangled in laughter's embrace,
In fashion's folly, we find our grace.

Tangled stories of fabric and seam,
In the tapestry of life, we laugh and dream.
Unravel the mess, spin tales around,
For every loose end, new joy is found.

The Sewn Path

In grandma's quilt, there's a hidden joke,
A patch that whispers – a mischievous poke.
Every stitch tells of fumbles and fun,
A wild bumblebee on a hot summer run.

A thimble named Larry, snug on my thumb,
Claims to be useful, but he's just so dumb.
In the needle's eye, adventures collide,
From fabric to fabric, we joyously glide.

Tangled yarn balls chase with a laugh,
Knitting a puzzle – my woolly gaffe.
Twisting and turning, a sock goes rogue,
In the land of the crafty, I'm just a toad.

Stitches unsewn, like tales left untold,
In every mishap, a memory we hold.
So we craft our quirks with laughter and cheer,
Sewing the moments we cherish each year.

Chronicles Interlaced

Oh, the saga of shoelaces gone wild,
Tangled and tripped, just like a child.
With one grand step while trying to race,
I end up twisted, a comedic disgrace.

A patchwork of laughter, a shirt gone wrong,
Who knew mismatched prints could be so strong?
Each color clashing like a choir out of tune,
A fashion faux pas that makes the room swoon.

A tale of the trousers that shrunk in the wash,
Now lovingly worn like a cozy, small posh.
In every wrinkle, surprises abound,
Making us giggle, salvation is found.

With every twist, a new story we spin,
Life's little mess-ups make room for the grin.
So let's wear our hiccups like badges of pride,
In the chronicles woven, we laugh and abide.

The Stitched Soul

Buttons are bouncing on the kitchen floor,
Frolicking freely, oh what a chore!
One leaps away like a rabbit in glee,
My wardrobe's circus, come watch and see!

A fabric softener with a fickle whim,
Makes clothes smell lovely, but pants are slim!
Caught in a whirlwind like socks on a spree,
Who knew my laundry would turn into glee?

A fabric tale spun in threads of delight,
The needle takes charge as we dance through the night.
With every misstep, more laughter will bloom,
As we sew up adventures to fill up the room.

So let's button up worries, let giggles unfurl,
In this quirky tapestry, let joy twirl!
Every stitch is a story, each seam a dare,
In the stitched soul of life, we find love everywhere.

Weaving Whispers

In a world where whispers dance,
Odd socks join the merry prance.
A tale spun from mismatched pairs,
Unraveling in the evening airs.

Caught in laughter, they collide,
As mismatched buttons choose a side.
The tales they weave, a curious fate,
Knitting chaos on a dinner plate.

A stitch of joy, a patch of glee,
Laughing cats in a patchwork spree.
With every knot, a giggle grows,
As silly stories spill from toes.

Grandma's cat, a threadbare sage,
Weaves yarn of love on every page.
In every whimper, a legend lies,
As socks take flight 'neath starlit skies.

Fragments of Fate

Once upon a time, oh dear,
A sandwich fell, the dog drew near.
It rolled and tumbled, a wild spree,
Each bite a twist of destiny.

Two pigeons squawked, intrigued by chance,
Their clumsy waltz, a funny dance.
A crumb, a prize, they fought to seize,
Creating chaos with cheeky ease.

In a park where stories bloom,
A squirrel erupted from the gloom.
He grabbed the loot, oh what a sight,
Then vanished quick in a flash of flight.

Yet every tale must find its end,
As fortunes shift, and laughter bends.
In life's great game of fate's caprice,
Even mischief finds a piece of peace.

Tapestry of Time

Time's a quilt made of silly threads,
With patches of laughter, and dreams in beds.
Each moment stitched with joy and strife,
A tapestry woven of whimsical life.

A catnap here, a misadventure there,
A table flipped, a somersault flare.
From morning coffee that made you trip,
To a rubber chicken's slippery quip.

Stitching memories with needles bright,
A flamboyant dance in the moon's soft light.
Old folks chuckle at tales they tell,
As time unwinds, casting its spell.

So grab a moment, twist it tight,
Turn it into pure delight.
In the patchwork bustle, we find our tune,
Each thread a laugh beneath the moon.

Silken Stitches of Memory

Once, a snail wore a shiny crown,
He'd glide through puddles, never drown.
With shimmering hopes stitched on his shell,
He ruled a realm where giggles dwell.

Acorns gathered with utmost glee,
Planning a party for the Bumblebee.
They danced all night with socks on hand,
In a silly world so wonderfully planned.

A mouse skated on a slice of cheese,
While squirrels cheered in the leafy breeze.
The tales spun round like a whirlgig's race,
A fiesta fueled by chuckles and grace.

Each stitch a whisper from times gone by,
Echoing laughter in the evening sky.
In the quilt of life, oh what a blend,
Where joy and humor never end.

Ties That Bind Us

In a town of capers and quirks,
A cat wore a hat as it lurks.
It danced on the street, bold and proud,
While the dogs in tuxedos clapped loud.

Grandma knit a sweater so grand,
It stretched like a rubber band.
She wore it to bingo, a sight to behold,
Her lucky yarn spun stories of gold.

The postman slipped on a banana peel,
And landed in a very odd wheel.
He laughed and he tossed bills in the air,
As neighbors cheered on without a care.

Together, they squabbled and jested,
While life's funny moments were tested.
Through laughter and mishaps, they find their way,
Connecting like odd socks on laundry day.

Woven Dreams

At night, the stars shave their beards,
While frogs croak out their silly weirds.
A hammock built from spaghetti strands,
Is swung by the gentle moon's hands.

In dreams, I fly on a pickle balloon,
While jellyfish jive to a funky tune.
They twirl on the breeze, not a care in sight,
As fireflies flash like disco lights.

I met a sock that had lost its pair,
It told silly jokes that floated in air.
It said that loneliness is not so grim,
When one can still dance on a whim.

With laughter, our dreams intertwine,
Creating a world that's simply divine.
In this odd land, we wander and roam,
Building our fun, sticky web of home.

A Seam of History

In a dusty attic where memories play,
Lies a suit made of chips – hip hip hooray!
It once danced at a party of gnomes,
Now it just dreams of past glittery homes.

Old maps reveal where the treasure's stored,
A pizza slice drawn with a fork and a sword.
Historians laugh at the curious lore,
Of knights on the run from a pigeon war.

With each tale woven, a stitch here and there,
A quilt of mishaps beyond compare.
The fabric of time is a patchwork delight,
A goofy parade in the warm summer night.

So gather the memory threads all around,
Wrap them in laughter, let joy be unbound.
In this seam of history, we find our place,
In a world that wears a funny, warm face.

Touches of Time

A tick-tock frog hops without a care,
While squirrels debate how to style their hair.
Each moment's a giggle, a smile, a tease,
As time gives a wink with the greatest of ease.

Baking cookies at midnight, what a swell idea,
Until the dough sings, "You're ruining my cheer!"
With floury mustaches and giggles galore,
They leave traces of mischief right out the door.

The clock strikes thirteen, what a curious hour,
As fairies play chess with a dandelion flower.
They toss about wishes like silly confetti,
While time giggles madly, "Oh, isn't this petty?"

In this whimsical dance, every second is bright,
A sprinkle of laughter in day and in night.
With soft touches of time, we weave and we jest,
Creating a tale that is simply the best.

A Quilt of Hearts

In a patchwork of giggles, we sew,
With colors so bright, they steal the show.
Each heart a square, stitched with care,
Who knew our madness could be so rare?

A frayed edge here, a spill from that,
A noodle from lunch caught in my hat.
With every loop, our laughter grows,
Creating chaos only friendship knows.

Bumbling and tumbling, we chase a thread,
Is that a string or a worm instead?
In this quilt, we cuddle, no need for pride,
Our funny mishaps the threads we ride.

So here's to stumbles, bumps, and blunders,
To crafting joy through silly wonders.
With every stitch, a tale to tell,
In a quilt of hearts, we all excel.

The Weft of Wishes

In a loom of dreams, we weave our fate,
With wishes afloat, never too late.
A twist here, a twirl there, oh what fun,
Each fiber a laugh, with stories spun.

A wish for a kiss, or maybe a donut,
We mix up the flavors like a bubbly soda.
When fabric breaches and we all gasp,
It's just our dreams in a binding clasp.

As threads intertwine, a pattern appears,
It's messy and wild, but we shed no tears.
We're adding a dash of silly to blend,
For in this design, the fun never ends.

So let's spin our wishes, see where they go,
On a magical carpet, we'll steal the show.
In the weft of hopes, we'll dance about,
With giggles and grins, it's never a drought.

Looming Legacies

In the fabric of life, we start with a thread,
A knot here and there, and off we sped.
Each moment's a stitch, a giggle or two,
Creating a legacy, funny and true.

From grandma's tales of the cat with a hat,
To uncle's mischief, that silly brat.
We stitch them together, laugh till we cry,
In this legacy loom, let the good times fly.

A fabric of folly, a quilt made of quirks,
With threads of our past, it really works.
We stitch up the laughter that echoes in time,
Looming with legends, all wrapped in rhyme.

So let's raise a toast to the gaffes and the glee,
In this tapestry woven, forever we'll be.
With each silly story, we're crafting a page,
In the loom of our lives, let's dance on this stage.

Stitching Together Silence

In a quiet corner, we gather the scraps,
Stitching together those awkward gaps.
A nod and a wink, then silence turns loud,
Crafting our joy, we feel so proud.

With needle in hand, we work with finesse,
Turning quiet moments into a mess.
A laugh bubbling up from a glance gone askew,
In stillness, the humor is never too few.

Threading the needle between the soft sighs,
We patch up the silence, oh what a surprise.
Each stitch a chuckle, a snicker or cackle,
Reinventing silence, what a fine tackle!

So when silence speaks, let's not run away,
We'll craft a new laugh in a quiet display.
In this tapestry made of our mutual cheer,
The laughter of silence is what we hold dear.

Fabric of Relationships

In the quilt of friends, patchwork smiles arise,
Each stitch a tale, where humor lies.
Laughter's the needle, sharp and bright,
Drawing us close, in day and night.

At the thrift shop, we find some socks,
Two lefts, no rights, just silly blocks.
Sewing mishaps, a button flies,
We roll on the floor, gasping for sighs.

Grandma's advice, with a wink and a nod,
Sew kindness in, but don't pull the fraud.
A tapestry woven with giggles and cheer,
In the fabric of life, we hold each dear.

Frayed edges of stories, a comical twist,
In stitches of joy, how could we resist?
With everything patched, it's fun we create,
In this crazy fabric, we celebrate fate.

The Woven Heart

With yarns of laughter, we knit tight and close,
Each purl a secret that nobody knows.
Frogged mistakes cause laughs in the night,
Our patterns twisted, yet just feel right.

Bob the cat steals the wool from our hands,
Unraveling dreams, just as he planned.
Knots of our mischief, we can't help but shout,
As we trip over fibers, there's no doubt!

Colors so bright, like our jokes on a roll,
But watch out for tangles that take their toll.
The woven heart beats with quirky delights,
In each happy stitch, our friendship ignites.

So grab your needles, let's craft the absurd,
In a canvas of joy, our voices are heard.
In this woven tale where we dance and we play,
The laughter we share makes dull moments sway.

The Sewn Narrative

Once was a seamstress with tales in her thread,
Stitching up worries, creating instead.
A patch for the past, a hem for tomorrow,
With chuckles and giggles, she turned every sorrow.

Her scissors were shears of joy and delight,
Snipping away troubles, oh what a sight!
She sewed in a cat that would dance on the floor,
Each leap and each pounce made us laugh more.

Errant buttons jumped like cheeky little bugs,
Finding their way into warm, cozy hugs.
Each story she crafted with loops and a spin,
Made all of us smile, under our skin.

In the sewn narrative, we find our way,
In stitches of laughter, we love and we play.
Life's quilt is forever, unique and divine,
With humor as fabric, it all will align.

Binding Threads of Fate

Once in a bazaar, a weaver named Lila,
Said life is a pattern, quite a fine villa.
With quirky designs and colors galore,
She stitched up her dreams through the shop's open door.

A rogue piece of fabric began to misbehave,
It shouted, "Oh no! I won't be a slave!"
With laughter around, it danced on the stand,
Asthreading each tale with a wobbly hand.

In the fabric of fate, luck spun with flair,
"Let's make it ridiculous," Lila declared.
With zigzags and polka dots swirled in a mix,
She taught us to laugh at life's quirky tricks.

So bind those bright threads, make a tapestry bold,
With gaffes and with giggles, a story retold.
The fibers of fate twirl in joy and in play,
We stitch together smiles, come what may.

The Sewn Together Life

In a world of mismatched shoes,
I wander in laughable hues.
Tangled yarn in a butterfly knot,
Each day's laughter, a stitch forgot.

Life's fabric, a patchwork of cheer,
Stitched by friends, oh so near.
Quirky tales in every fold,
Embellished dreams, laughter bold.

The seams of mischief, they fray,
We trip on stories day by day.
A belt of blunders, it fits so tight,
But we wear it with pure delight!

Hints of a Journey

With every step, I tiptoe bold,
Map in hand, but I'm often told,
That up ahead, I might just fall,
The sign says 'trip', forgotten at all.

A bus ride with socks that don't match,
The driver's jokes, a friendly hatch.
Crumbs from crackers scatter and fly,
As laughter transports us through the sky.

Lost in the forest of candy trees,
We dance with squirrels, do as we please.
Every bump on the road, a comical twist,
On this journey, how could I resist?

Mosaic of Moments

Little bits of laughter stuck,
In a jar, we have bad luck.
Mom's pie gets stuck on the roof,
The cat pounces—missing proof!

A mosaic made of silly frights,
Dancing with socks on summer nights.
Each memory glued with gum and tape,
In a quirky, laugh-filled shape.

A sprinkle of 'oops' and 'did you see?',
Life's funny screw-ups, wild and free.
From sprouting plants to awkward falls,
Together we giggle through it all!

The Needle's Dance

With a wobble and jig, the needle prances,
Stitching tales while everyone glances.
It twirls through fabric with glee and flair,
Leaving trails of laughter in the air.

Sewing patches of dumb luck here,
Each poke and prod, we shed a tear.
Moments stitched with a happy grin,
In the waltz of life where joy begins.

As threads go zigzag, sometimes they tangle,
A dance so funny, we're left to wrangle.
With each errant loop and vibrant spin,
The needle's dance makes the chuckles win!

The Mentor's Tapestry

In a cafe, I took my seat,
A mentor's tales, oh what a treat!
He spun yarns about his grand mistakes,
As laughter rose, my coffee shakes.

He spoke of socks and tangled threads,
Of knitting needles, and one-eyed beds.
Each stitch he missed was quite a tale,
In his world, chaos wore a veil.

The wrinkles in his face held dreams,
Of misadventures, wild and extreme,
He laughed at buttons lost in wars,
Turning fabric woes to mighty roars.

With humor stitched in every seam,
Life felt silly, like a dream.
We parted ways, yet kept the thread,
For every laugh he saw ahead.

The Stitch Beneath Time's Surface

Amidst the seams of time I snicker,
Finding patterns that grew thicker.
Each tick of the clock, a little joke,
Daydreams woven, thoughts that poke.

Grandma's quilt had stories to share,
Of a cat that thought it was a bear.
With every patch and funny font,
She'd mimic voices, oh what a daunt!

Invisible stitches, whispers arise,
Telling secrets under the skies.
A sock lost here, a shoe misplaced,
Time laughs with twists, never disgraced.

In life's big fabric, colors clash,
Funny moments that come in a flash.
I'll keep on laughing, it's quite a thrill,
As stitches form and the tales distill.

Weaving Whispers

In a cozy nook with laughter bright,
I weave my whispers, day and night.
Each laugh a loop, each joy a thread,
Mending memories, not much dread.

The cat walks by, a furry muse,
Leaving tufts that I can't refuse.
I knit them in with every guffaw,
Creating purrs, it's quite the law.

Neighbors peek and join the fun,
As stories spill, like rivers run.
With every stitch, we blend and bend,
What starts as yarn, becomes a friend.

Amid the fibers, giggles grow,
In tangles new, let laughter flow.
So join this quilt with joy and cheer,
In every stitch, the world feels near.

Stitches of Time

Upon the canvas of days gone by,
I stitch together moments, oh my!
A mishap here, a goof-up there,
Each patch a memory I cherish, I swear!

I crafted a clock with a silly face,
Ticking loudly, at a frantic pace.
Its hands were busy telling jokes,
To remind me of laughter in life's folks.

Mismatched socks and fading hues,
A story unravels, oh such views!
Twists and turns in life's grand spool,
Each mistake, I proudly call cool.

With every loop, I flip the script,
A tapestry of giggles, oddly equipped.
So let's create, with yarn and glee,
Stitches of time, just you and me!

Encounters in Embroidery

In a jumble of colors, we stitched quite a mess,
A cat snatched my needle, oh what a distress!
Grandma's watching, her eyes full of glee,
"Just look at you both! What a sight to see!"

The thread went awry, and we laughed 'til we cried,
A tapestry forming, with joy as our guide.
An errant stitch turned into a cat,
Now it's an artwork! How silly is that?

Who knew that the fabric could unravel so well,
A quilt of mishaps, with stories to tell.
We spun a great yarn, with laughter and cheer,
In this embroidery, the fun stayed near.

So here's to our meeting, our needles in hand,
Each knot a new venture, so carefully planned.
With every new loop, our laughter will soar,
In this silly adventure, who could ask for more?

Narrative Fibers

Wool and cotton, a twist and a turn,
Every fiber singing; oh, how they yearn!
A sock that turned blue, and a scarf that went red,
Mixed-up intentions? Who's tangled in thread?

My friend sneezed loud, it was rather a sight,
A yarn ball rolled away, oh what a fright!
Chasing down wool with a giggle and dash,
We tangled our lives in a colorful splash.

Purls and stitches, we clumsily knit,
These narrative fibers? Not one will fit!
But laughter prevails; it's a tale to embrace,
A memoir of yarn that sits in its place.

So here we gather, with needles in hand,
Creating a tale that we never planned.
Each loop and each twist, a memory made,
In this funky adventure where laughter won't fade!

In the Loop of Time

Tick tock, said the clock, as we spun round and round,
A circle of yarn, oh what chaos we found!
With every new loop, we might fall on our seat,
As laughter erupts over tangled old feet.

Time flies when you're crafting, or so it is said,
But this loop is a monster with threads bright and red.
We're caught in the rhythm of needles and giggles,
Dancing through time with our joyous wriggles.

"Oh dear, what's this?" a knot shaped like fate,
We'll untie it with humor, it's never too late!
With every mishap, a story unfolds,
In the loop of our laughter, our tales are retold.

So here we are, friends, in this merry affair,
With yarn around our fingers, and time in the air.
Each stitch takes a moment, each laugh writes the rhyme,
In this playful endeavor, we're one with the time!

The Weave of Affection

In a tapestry woven with warmth and with care,
Threads cross and mingle; it's all quite a pair!
A neighbor once borrowed, my best yarn, oh dear,
Now my mittens look funny, but they bring me good cheer!

Every stitch holds a tale, with giggles entwined,
A scarf full of memories, with laughter aligned.
Well-meaning hands in this crafty pursuit,
Creating a masterpiece that's utterly cute.

And when we're together, our hearts weave and flow,
Mismatched creations that shine with a glow.
Oh look at this mess, a hat squeaks with flair,
Each pattern a memory, we gladly declare!

So let's raise our needles and spin out the fun,
In this weave of affection, we're never outdone.
With threads that are silly, and laughter that lasts,
Together we stitch, creating our past!

The Fabric of Narratives

Once a tale began with a blunder,
A sock lost in the laundry's thunder.
It told of dragons, a hero's plight,
But mostly about a cat's late-night bite.

With each twist and turn, the plot would fray,
A squirrel stole the gold on a fateful day.
The knight chased his lunch, missed the grand feast,
Wound up with a pie, a savory beast.

And as the bard wove his yarn so tight,
He tripped on his lute in the dim candlelight.
The laughter echoed, the tales took flight,
Turning heartache to giggles, a true delight.

So take a seat, hear this quirky tale,
Of mishaps and mix-ups, we shall prevail.
In the fabric of narratives, joy's the best thread,
Stitching smiles with every word that's said.

Strings of Destiny

In a land where shoelaces danced all day,
A clown tripped over the jester's bouquet.
They tied knots of fate, then lost their own shoes,
While a squirrel in a hat refused to snooze.

A wizard tried to fix a broken broom,
But ended up spinning around the room.
With each crazy spell, the chaos would grow,
Turning pumpkins to coaches—bam!—off they go!

An ogre, not fierce, but quite fond of pie,
Cried out, "Oh dear! I'm too full to fly!"
His friends rolled with laughter, what a sight to see,
In the game of their lives, no one plays for free.

So spin the yarn, let the giggles take hold,
Through whimsical twists, new tales unfold.
For in every stumble, hiccup, and turn,
There's laughter to gather, and love you can earn.

Interwoven Lives

Two friends embarked on a quest one day,
To find the best cupcake in the town's café.
They mixed up the orders, what a great mess,
One got a donut, the other—no less!

A cat with a hat and a cheese-loving mouse,
Joined in the fun, turned the cafe to a house.
They baked and they laughed, flour flew in the air,
While the baker looked on with a glint and a stare.

A bard joined the fray, strumming a tune,
While dancing on tables under the moon.
Breads turned to bagpipes, cookies to drums,
It turned into chaos, yet oh how it hums!

So play on, dear friends, create your own vibe,
A party in laughter, all aches they imbibe.
Interwoven lives bloom in quirky array,
In every mishap, there's magic at play.

Echoes in the Loom

In the loom of life, the stitches went wild,
An elephant danced, oh my, how he smiled!
His trunk waved like a wand, he twirled around,
While mice in top hats played music profound.

A story unfolded, with giggles in layers,
As the bard sang of pirates—devil-may-cares.
Their sabers were forks, their ships made of cheese,
They conquered the cupcakes with effortless ease.

Then the dragon showed up, with a sneeze and a roar,
But the humor was rich, and the laughter would soar.
He chased after dancers in a frothy delight,
Only to trip on a banana peel—what a sight!

So weave your own magic, let laughter ensue,
In the echoes of stories where whimsy is true.
The loom spins stories, oh what a grand game,
In each playful moment, there's joy without shame.

Threads of Yesterday

Once I found a sock, so lost and alone,
It danced with its twin, on the floor, like a drone.
They argued of colors, of patterns and stripes,
While I brewed a laugh, oh those quirky gripes.

In the back of the closet, they plotted their scheme,
To escape to the laundry, oh what a dream!
With a leap and a spin, they grabbed hold of a cat,
Who simply was baffled, like 'What's up with that?'

I joined in their antics, we played peek-a-boo,
A trio of mischief, now what could we do?
We wove through the house like a parade of jest,
While mom yelled, 'Stay still! You're a terrible mess!'

In the end, we surrendered, all tangled and fun,
The socks made their peace, their wild dance was done.
Underneath the couch, they found their last stop,
Where I learned some laughs never really do drop.

Twisted Tales

In a town with a cat who wore socks on her paws,
She roamed with a flair, defying all laws.
She'd tell silly stories to all of her friends,
While knitting a cap as the laughter transcends.

A dog joined the fray, with a couple of tails,
He wagged as he listened to whimsical tales.
They plotted each night for a grand midnight show,
And the neighbors would gather, no one cared who'd know.

From dragons to robots, each night brought a twist,
As the audience roared, who could ever resist?
But one fateful night, the punchlines went flew,
And the cat lost a sock—oh the horror that grew!

But laughter flowed freely and friends held her tight,
They wore wacky socks, celebrating the night.
So the moral is clear, keep your stories alive,
For a twist in the tale makes the laughter survive.

The Seamstress's Silent Song

Eliza the seamstress had needles galore,
With thread that danced brightly, her secrets in store.
She stitched the whole town into outfits so grand,
While humming a tune, with a needle in hand.

The mayor, now dressed like a clown at the fair,
With polka dot pants and a bright purple pair.
The townsfolk all giggled, the children, they roared,
As Eliza just smiled, her laughter ignored.

One day she decided to sew up a cake,
With fabric for frosting, oh what a mistake!
The guests took a bite, then choked on their prints,
As laughter erupted from all of their hints.

Yet Eliza just chuckled, with a wink and a nod,
Her fashion faux pas was her joyful facade.
In the end, laughter stitched all that she made,
For life is much sweeter when fun's not delayed.

Unraveled Narratives

A tale of old Isaac, who lived in a street,
Whose stories unraveled at a comical beat.
He'd spin yarns of pirates who sailed in a shoe,
And grinned with delight as the punchlines just grew.

One day while he chatted, his cat took a leap,
And knocked over yarn, oh the trouble was steep!
The pirates went flying, the treasure was lost,
As chaos erupted, who thought of the cost?

His neighbor named Sally just couldn't contain,
Her laughter erupted like a runaway train.
She joined him in antics, with tales of her own,
Together they crafted a narrative grown!

By the end of the day, they were tangled in fun,
With stories so silly, they counted as one.
So here's to the laughter that weaves us so tight,
In the fabric of friendship, where stories unite.

The Quilt of Unspoken Words

In a patchwork of silence, we grin,
A fabric of whispers, where secrets begin.
Each square holds a giggle, a blush or two,
Stitched tight with laughter, all stitched in blue.

Grandma's old quilt, a most curious sight,
With cats and with clowns, it's quite a delight.
We hide all our doubts under layers so neat,
While cheery old stories dance on our feet.

The corners are frayed, like Grandpa's big jokes,
They come out at family reunions, like folks.
With each vibrant patch, a memory unfurls,
In this quilt of laughter, we're all just like squirrels.

So here's to the threads that bind us in cheer,
With each stitch we make, we hold memories dear.
In this colorful blanket, we find our own bliss,
And who knows, maybe stitch a laugh or a kiss!

Mosaic of Moments

A jigsaw of giggles, a collage of fun,
In this wacky world, we shine like the sun.
Moments like pixels in a wild dance,
Each one is a story, a silly romance.

With breadcrumbs of joy, on the path that we tread,
We trip over laughter, it's all in our head.
Falling like dominoes, we roll on the floor,
Collecting our moments, always wanting more.

From birthday balloons to a frog in a hat,
Each piece tells a tale; oh, where are we at?
Flip-flops and fortune cookies join the spree,
This mosaic's alive, just like you and me.

So savor each chuckle, each wobbly twist,
In this artwork of life, it's too grand to miss.
Constructing our story, artfully true,
With every quirk and mishap, we're stitched right on through.

Braided Fates

Three strands intertwine, what a tangled mess,
In this tale of our lives, we find some duress.
With each twist and turn, we chuckle and fight,
For misadventures surely make wrong feel right.

From baker to bungee, we wear many hats,
We trip on our dreams like a herd of fat cats.
Life's knots may feel tight, but we laugh with glee,
For who knew that chaos could set us all free?

Twirling like dancers, we each take a turn,
With belly laughs bubbling, we joyfully burn.
Each strand has a story, a mishap or two,
As we weave through the tapestry, all bright and askew.

So here's to our braids, full of kooky delight,
With humor as strong as our bond feels so tight.
Together we laugh, though it sometimes looks strange,
For in this wild dance, we'll always exchange.

A Yarn of Hope

Spinning our tales like a cat with some thread,
With curious antics that dance in our head.
Each knot tells a story, each twist holds a dream,
Life's a fuzzy yarn, a ridiculous theme.

With colors so bright, like a clown at a fair,
We toss in the chaos, with sparkle and flair.
From the wildest of wishes to dandelion puffs,
This yarn keeps unraveling, but never enough!

From the snags of our lives, we create a design,
With laughter in stitches, our lives intertwine.
With every good giggle, we grow a new stitch,
In this yarn of hope, we're all quite a glitch.

So knit it all up, with a wink and a sigh,
In this tapestry snug, let's continue to fly.
For every moment matters, every laugh rings true,
In the yarn of our lives, it's just me and you!

www.ingramcontent.com/pod-product-compliance
Lightning Source LLC
Chambersburg PA
CBHW060116230426
43661CB00003B/203